T0290517

SOYBEAN TRADING and HEDGING
USING GRANDMILL'S EXCLUSIVE PRICE AND TIMING TABLES

© Copyright 1984 by Wm. Grandmill Ltd.

© Copyright 1987 by William Grandmill

Published by Windsor Books
P.O. Box 280
Brightwaters, N.Y. 11718

PART 1
HOW TO BUY
SOYBEANS
SAFELY and PROFITABLY

WHAT KIND OF TRADING METHOD IS THIS?

In a word — **conservative.** Trading methods vary in risk from one extreme to another. On one extreme, the most rash and risky type of trading would be one where a speculator with only enough money for the margin would buy corn, for example, with a margin of $500 and use a stop of 3 or 4 cents. The chance of survival is small.

The other extreme would be one where it is almost impossible to lose all one's capital. An example of which would be a situation where the trader would put up an amount of capital equal to the total value of the commodity. For example, if corn was $2.50 a bushel, and if he thought corn prices were going to rise, the trader's initial capital outlay would be $12,500 (5000 bu. × $2.50), and he would buy **one** contract without using a stop. Even if prices went temporarily against him, even falling away below the loan rate (the worst case, by the way, was a drop of 41¢ below the loan rate), the trader would still be in the market and would show a profit eventually. If he earned the average corn profit (about $2500), he would have realized a profit of about 20% on his capital. That's better than bonds but not as safe. All commodity trading contains an element of risk, no matter how careful one becomes. The object is to reduce the risk to a minimum. However, this method is being rejected because it requires too much money. Later, you will learn a method which is just as safe, requires much less capital, and earns a larger percentage of profit.

The best solution lies between the two extremes mentioned above. The trading method outlined here is not exactly half-way between the two extremes; instead, it is situated more toward the conservative end of the scale.

This method of trading will stress the following —
The safety and preservation of capital — At all costs, a trader's capital must be protected from loss. Once one's money is lost, all hope of success is also lost. This method stresses safety and the avoidance of risk.

Starting with adequate capital — Any exprienced trader will tell you that there is no point in initiating a commodity position in the first place if you do not have enough money to see it through to a successful conclusion. Trying to get by with a minimum of capital is almost always unsuccessful. Your capital will consist of two parts; the margin and some back-up money in case your position goes against you. For example, let's say the margin for buying soybeans is $1500. In addition to the margin, you should have an additional amount of $3000, for example, as back-up capital in case you got into the market before the bottom. Very few commodity positions go smoothly in the desired direction without some hitch or reversal. You must be prepared to ride out a temporary reversal. But how would one know how much extra money may be needed? A table of soybean prices later in the book will provide the answer. It is called the Low Protective Price Table. Its use will be explained later. This method, then, is based on the premise that you must have adequate capital to trade successfully.

Trading without the use of a stop — This method recommends that you do not use a stop in the early stages of your position — use adequate capital instead. This may sound like unusual advice, but if you think back to all the times you have used a stop when buying grain or soybeans, you will likely find that stops have done more harm than good. Nearly everyone has some horror stories of how, when he went long and placed a stop at a few cents below his entry price, the market came down and just touched his stop, then proceeded in the desired direction, leaving him out of the market. Stops have a way of being touched — almost deliberately, some traders believe. Later, you will learn that this method uses a stop, but it is used to protect a profit which has already been made.

Trading long term — This method is suitable for long term trading. It is not suited for "day trading". A working person should trade long term. Anyone who trades short term must be in a position where he can phone his broker several times a day. Most professional and working people are not in a position to do so. A working person should be able to go about his work free from anxiety, not worrying whether he may get a margin call. Adequate capital and long term trading cut down on stress. However, in return for safety of capital and for stress-free trading, one must be prepared to accept a lower percentage of profit than one might get in a risky position. Lower risk and lower profits usually go together.

CORN and SOYBEAN RELATIONSHIPS

There are four concepts to be explained before the trading method is discussed.

The first concept — This refers to the relationship between corn prices and soybean prices. A bullish bias in one will usually affect the other. If corn prices are bullish and begin to move upward, they will likely pull soybean prices up along with them. A correlation exists between corn prices and soybean prices. This correlation will be used to help estimate the high of the prices for the soybean crop year.

The second concept — This refers to the carryover of soybeans and corn at the end of the crop year. The carryover is converted into a percent-of-total-use ratio (carryover divided by total use × 100 = %). This percentage number tells us something. For example, we can safely say that an estimated carryover of 10% for soybeans will likely be more bullish for prices than a carryover of 25%. In other words, the size of the carryover will have an important bearing on how high soybean prices will rise in the coming crop year. USDA puts out a crop report in October. Use the data from that report to estimate the carryover for the coming crop year which will end on the next Aug. 31st. Because the year's low soybean price usually occurs at harvest time, the October report comes at just the right time to go long in beans. Ask your broker for that report.

The third concept — This refers to the economy. Throughout the coming crop year, soybean prices will be affected by economic conditions, weather, foreign crop conditions, strength of the U.S. dollar abroad, etc. These external factors can change the price expectations, regardless of the size of the carryover. This book attempts to deal with that problem. It is realized that the method used here would not stand up to professional scrutiny, but it is better than doing nothing at all. We can't pretend the problem doesn't exist. The method here is quick, easy to use, and the results of these external factors will be used to adjust the soybean price structure.

The fourth concept — This refers to the highest post-harvest soybean price. There is a price which can be expected to be the highest soybean price of the crop year when you take into account the size of the carryover, the inter-relationship of the corn and soybean prices, and the economic, weather factors mentioned above. All these factors play a part in determining how high bean prices will go.

All these concepts are incorporated into the following tables of soybean prices.

ON THE FOLLOWING PAGES —

You will see one page of indicators for the economy, weather etc. You will also see three pairs of tables dealing with soybean prices.

Please look at the page of indicators. You will see that each group has a point rating — e.g. from +10 to -10 points. You will evaluate each group by selecting the most appropriate line, and note its point value. Having gone through all the groups, you will total the points selected to obtain a total point value. You will rate your total point value on the rating scale to obtain an answer to this question: **Are conditions good or average or poor for a rise in soybean prices?** That answer (good, average, or poor) will determine which of the three pairs of price tables you will use — more details on this later.

Conditions will change as the crop year progresses. The soil moisture will change, also the economy, strength of the U.S. dollar, the bullish consensus, etc. To keep up to date, it is best to go through the page of indicators once a month. This means that the estimated highest price for the year will change; and that is the way it should be. Changing conditions change the price structure. Your broker should be able to supply you with any of the information needed for this page.

Some of the point values may puzzle you. Look at the Soil Moisture group, and you will see that "ideal conditions" is valued at -5. Why? Because this means an excellent yield can be expected, which will increase supplies, which will be negative for prices. Look at the Bullish Consensus. Why, when 80% of the traders are bullish, would it be valued at -10? Answer: According to the bullish consensus theory, the price trend will change from up to down when 80% are bullish because the market is overbought.

Please look at the first page of price tables. You will see two tables. The top one is "Soybean's Estimated Highest Price Tables — nearest month — Under Good Conditions". This is the page you would choose when the Indicator Page showed that the economy, weather etc. were signalling "Good Conditions", which means that soybean prices would be very bullish and would likely rise higher than average.

Look at the left column, and you will see that the numbers represent "Soybean's Estimated Carryover as %". Look at the bottom row, and you will see "Corn's Estimated Carryover As % Of Total Use". By using the two percentage carryover numbers, we can find the estimated highest price for the crop year, **under good conditions. Example:** Let's say the date is Nov. 1st, 198?. The data from USDA's October crop report was used, and it indicated a carryover at the end of the crop year next fall of 12% for soybeans, and 19% for corn. You think the bean prices have bottomed and it is time to think of going long. Using the Highest Price tables and the percent carryovers of 12% for beans (the left column) and 19% for corn (the bottom row) you find $9.00 at the place where the two converge. (Follow this in the tables) That means, that with the best of conditions in the economy, foreign crop conditions, etc., we can expect the highest soybean price to be about $9.00

To continue the same example further, let's say that you are thinking of buying July soybeans which closed today at $7.20. With a likely high coming up of $9.00, you can see that the trade should be very profitable. You decide to go long July beans, **without using a stop,** because you will have adequate capital instead. The question now is. "How much extra money over the margin do you need in order to have 'adequate capital'?" The answer will be found in the table below, at the bottom of the page. It is called "Soybean's Low Protective Price Table — Under Good Conditions". This table will tell you how far you should cover your position, to what low price, so that you will be trading safely.

To continue with the same example; you wish to know how much extra capital will be needed to protect the long July bean position to a safe level, a price low enough that it is almost certain never to be touched under the present good conditions. Let's find that low protective price. Using the percent carryover of 12% for beans and 19% for corn, we find the low price is $5.80 in this table. That means that you should have enough extra money to cover your position from the entry price of $7.20 to the protective price of $5.80. That means that you should have $7000 as back-up capital. ($7.20 - $5.80 = $1.40 which is $7000). That sounds like a lot of money — and it is. But it does not mean that you should hand over $7000 to your broker. It means that you should have the money available, in the bank, in bonds earning interest. Just having it handy will give you a secure feeling and peace of mind. Only about $2000 should be put into your commodity account as a start. Remember, we are dealing here with one of the most volatile agricultural products. With modest back-up capital of $1500, for example, you would need luck to survive. If a position is worth taking in the first place, it is worth protecting.

Look at the next pair of tables. These are the ones you would use if the indicator page showed that conditions were **average.** The tables are used the same way as the previous pair. The prices in the tables are different from the previous pair which were "under good conditions".

Look at the last pair of tables. They are to be used when conditions are **poor** for a rise in soybean prices. They are used the same way as shown in the previous example.

5

Another Example — (Follow this in the tables) The time is Dec. 1st and you have thought of going long in July soybeans. July beans are now at $5.70. Using the latest USDA data, you find the carryover for soybeans is 15%, the carryover for corn is 36%. (1) Use the **indicator page** of influencing factors. For this example, let the conditions be **average.** (2) that means that you will use the second set of tables, which use the words **"Under Average Conditions".** (3) Using the percentage carryovers of 15% for beans and 36% for corn in the top table, you get an estimated highest price for the crop year of $6.60 (4) Using the **low protective price table,** you get $5.05. (5) You buy July soybeans at $5.70. (6) You will need $3250 as extra back-up capital to protect your position to the low protective price of $5.05, in addition to the margin. (7) You hold that one position to maturity, without using a stop. When is maturity? When the price peaks — which could be later than July, which means that you may wish to roll the contract over into the September contract. However, in **average** conditions, the peak usually occurs before July.

HOW TO ADD A SECOND POSITION

As mentioned previously, this is a conservative method of trading. One position will be enough for some people. But there will also be some traders who would like to add on another soybean position, using the same amount of capital on hand for the first position. In other words, if you wish, you may take another position without having to put up any more money. But it has to be done in a safe, cautious way.

Let's assume the following has happened: You have taken your first position, without using a stop but with adequate capital. Now for the new steps: (1) when prices have risen more than 30¢ above the entry price, place a stop about 5¢ above the entry price. For example, if you had entered the position at $6.00, and prices had gone in your favor to $6.35, then you can place a stop at $6.05 to protect your trade. (2) This will now free your extra back-up capital, and it can be used again as though you were going to take another first position. In this example, you may buy another soybean contract at $6.35, without a stop, and use the back-up money for the new position. If the worst happened, and prices declined a lot, the first position would be stopped out at a small profit, and the extra capital would be protecting the last position taken. (3) Later you may again wish to re-take that stopped-out position so that you will have two of them. In this example, you would not take it until prices had risen over 30¢ above the present position — which means that you would re-take the second one at about $6.70, and place a stop at $6.40 to protect the first trade. (4) What is happening is this: no new position should be taken until the first one is protected with a stop about 5¢ above the entry price. This way, your extra capital is being used to protect only **one** position at all times. Actually, it may be possible to take a third position but only if you follow the rules outlined in the next paragraph.

The 40% line — Rule: the second and third new position must be taken in the lower 40% of the price rise. **Now for an explanation.** When you buy July soybeans, for example, you are naturally trying to get in at or near the bottom price, likely in the late fall. Let's suppose you buy July beans at $6.00. You will use the % carryovers to find the estimated highest price from the tables. Let's suppose it was $8.00. Thus, there is an estimated possible $2 price move to be made, the difference between the entry price of $6.00 and the estimated highest price of $8.00. Here is where the rule applies: in this example, you must complete the buying of the second and third positions below $6.80. Why at $6.80? Because $6.80 is at 40% of the difference between the entry price and the estimated highest price of $8.00. ($8 - $6 = $2, 40% of $2 = 80¢, $6.00 + 80¢ = $6.80). All buying should be completed below the 40% line.

Why this rule? Answer: to stay out of trouble. The top half of a bull move always has more price turbulence and problems than the bottom half. You are usually in a safe area in the bottom half of a big move. Your profit and back-up capital are at more risk in the top half of the profit area. Play it safe by not taking any new positions in that risky area.

TAKING YOUR PROFITS — how to get out

It seems to be as difficult to get out of a long position in soybeans, as it is to get into one. Ultimately, it is your own judgement that will prevail. You must make the decision. The object is to make as much profit as possible, but waiting for the last cent can be costly. The suggestions below should help.

1. Have a predetermined price in mind, and get out of the position at or near that price.
2. This book offers you two distinct methods of estimating the top price for the crop year. These two methods are completely independent of each other — so you have two different estimates. One method uses tables which are oriented to cycles and the price structure. The other makes use of the interrelationship with corn.
3. Timing. Make use of the estimated timing of the high or low from the timing tables.
4. Get out of the market when **one** of the goals is reached: the timing goal **or** the price goal. Don't wait for both to coincide — they may not do so.
5. You may make use of such technical aids as: moving averages, the relative strength index, the bullish consensus, etc.
6. Make use of a trailing stop. It works like this: as the estimated highest price comes close, place a stop at about 6¢ below the last close price. If the price moves up the next day, move the stop up as well. Continue with this manoeuvre until you are stopped out. The idea behind a trailing stop is this: the stop will protect a profit already made, and if there is to be any more money to be made by prices going up, you are taking advantage of that price rise while, at the same time, you are protecting yourself against a downward move. This is a good, legitimate use of a stop: to protect a profit that is already made.
7. Pay attention to the top and low price estimates in a newsletter or from your brokerage house.
8. Be alert to important news, such as a report of a large soybean crop in Brazil which would put a cap on any upward price movement in the soybean futures market.

SOYBEAN PRICE INDICATORS

SOYBEAN CARRYOVER

carryover	points
5%	+20
10%	+10
15%	0
20%	-5
25%	-10

NEXT CROP ACRES TO BE PLANTED

% change	points
20% more	-20
10% more	-1-
same	0
10% less	+10
20% less	+20

BRAZIL'S EXPECTED NEW CROP (in million tonnes)

crop size	points
16+m.t.	-15
15 m.t.	-8
14 m.t.	0
13 m.t.	+8
12 m.t.	+15

STRENGTH OF U.S. DOLLAR

strength	points
very weak	+10
weak	+5
average	0
strong	-5
very strong	-10

INFLATION RATE

size	points
0%	-5
5%	0
10%	+4
15%	+8
20%	+10

FOREIGN CROP CONDITIONS (Russia, China, W. Europe avg.)

condition	points
good	-8
average	0
poor	+10

CORN CARRYOVER

carryover	points
5%	+10
10%	+8
15%	+3
20%	-3
25%	-5
30%	-7
35%	-9

SOIL MOISTURE

condition	points
damaging wet	+10
wet	+5
normal	0
ideal	-5
dry	+7
drought	+30

ECONOMY

condition	points
recession	-10
slow down	-5
average	0
up turn	+5
good times	+10

BULLISH CONSENSUS

percentage	points
80%	-10
70%	-5
60%	0
50%	0
40%	0
30%	+5
20%	+10

RATE THE TOTAL POINTS HERE

total	comment	which tables to use
+30+	very bullish	Use "under good condition" tables
+20	bullish	Use "under good conditions" tables
+10	mildly bullish	Use "under average conditions" tables
0	average	Use "under average conditions" tables
-10	mildly bearish	Use "under average conditions" tables
-20	bearish	Use "under poor conditions" tables
-30-	very bearish	Use "under poor conditions" tables

BUYING SOYBEANS
USE THE TABLES ON THIS PAGE WHEN CONDITIONS ARE
GOOD FOR A RISE IN SOYBEAN PRICES

AN EXAMPLE using these tables —

1. Let's suppose the points from the indicator page totaled 22 — therefore the "under good conditions" tables are used.
2. Let's suppose the estimated soybean carryover for the end of the crop year on next Aug. 31st is 15%.
3. Let's suppose the estimated corn carryover for the end of the corn crop year on next Sep. 30th is 18%.
4. Using these percentages on the first table, we get an estimated highest soybean price for the crop year of $8.25.
5. From the bottom table, we get an estimated low protective price of $5.55.
6. Let's suppose that you had bought soybeans at $6.55. You will need $5000 available as back-up capital in addition to the margin, and you can expect a potential profit of about $8000 in this example.

SOYBEAN'S ESTIMATED HIGHEST PRICE TABLES
— nearest month — UNDER GOOD CONDITIONS

SOYBEAN'S ESTIMATED CARRYOVER AS %													
23 - 26	$8.00	$7.60	$7.25	$7.00	$6.75	$6.55	$6.40	$6.20	$6.00	$5.85	$5.75	$5.65	$5.55
20 - 23	8.50	8.10	7.75	7.45	7.20	7.00	6.80	6.60	6.40	6.25	6.15	6.05	5.95
17 - 20	9.10	8.65	8.10	7.85	7.65	7.45	7.25	7.05	6.90	6.80	6.70	6.60	6.50
14 - 17	9.80	9.30	8.95	8.55	8.25	8.00	7.80	7.65	7.50	7.40	7.30	7.20	7.10
11 - 14	10.60	10.10	9.70	9.30	9.00	8.80	8.60	8.40	8.25	8.10	8.00	7.90	7.80
8 - 11	11.50	10.95	10.50	10.10	9.80	9.60	9.40	9.20	9.05	8.90	8.80	8.70	8.60
5 - 8%	12.50	11.90	11.40	11.00	10.70	10.50	10.30	10.10	9.95	9.80	9.70	9.60	9.50
	5 - 8%	**8 - 11**	**11 - 14**	**14 - 17**	**17 - 20**	**20 - 23**	**23 - 26**	**26 - 29**	**29 - 32**	**32 - 35**	**35 - 38**	**38 - 41**	**41 - 44**

CORN'S ESTIMATED CARRYOVER AS % OF TOTAL USE

SOYBEAN'S LOW PROTECTIVE PRICE — UNDER GOOD CONDITIONS

SOYBEAN'S ESTIMATED CARRYOVER AS %													
23 - 26	$5.35	$5.25	$5.20	$5.15	$5.10	$5.05	$5.00	$4.95	$4.90	$4.85	$4.80	$4.75	$4.70
20 - 23	5.45	5.35	5.30	5.25	5.20	5.15	5.10	5.05	5.00	4.95	4.90	4.85	4.80
17 - 20	5.60	5.50	5.45	5.40	5.35	5.30	5.25	5.20	5.15	5.10	5.05	5.00	4.95
14 - 17	5.80	5.70	5.65	5.60	5.55	5.50	5.45	5.40	5.35	5.30	5.25	5.20	5.15
11 - 14	6.05	5.95	5.90	5.85	5.80	5.75	5.70	5.65	5.60	5.55	5.50	5.45	5.40
8 - 11	6.40	6.30	6.20	6.15	6.10	6.05	6.00	5.95	5.90	5.85	5.80	5.75	5.70
5 - 8%	6.85	6.70	6.60	6.50	6.45	6.40	6.35	6.30	6.25	6.20	6.15	6.10	6.05
	5 - 8%	**8 - 11**	**11 - 14**	**14 - 17**	**17 - 20**	**20 - 23**	**23 - 26**	**26 - 29**	**29 - 32**	**32 - 35**	**35 - 38**	**38 - 41**	**41 - 44**

CORN'S ESTIMATED CARRYOVER AS % OF TOTAL USE

BUYING SOYBEANS
USE THE TABLES ON THIS PAGE WHEN CONDITIONS ARE AVERAGE FOR A RISE IN SOYBEAN PRICES

AN EXAMPLE using these tables —

1. Let's suppose the points from the indicator page totaled -3. Therefore the "under average conditions" tables are used.
2. Let's suppose the estimated soybean carryover at the end of the crop year next Aug. 31st is 18%.
3. Let's suppose the estimated corn carryover at the end of the corn crop year next Sep. 30th is 22%.
4. Using the percentages on the top table, we get an estimated soybean highest price for the crop year of $6.95.
5. Using the bottom table, you get an estimated low protective price of $5.15.
6. Let's suppose that you bought soybeans at $6.05. Then you will need $4500 as back-up capital, in addition to the margin, and you can expect a potential profit of $4500 in this example.

SOYBEAN'S ESTIMATED HIGHEST PRICE TABLES
— nearest month — UNDER AVERAGE CONDITIONS

SOYBEAN'S ESTIMATED CARRYOVER AS %													
23 - 26	$7.80	$7.45	$7.15	$6.90	$6.70	$6.50	$6.30	$6.10	$5.95	$5.80	$5.65	$5.55	$5.50
20 - 23	7.95	7.60	7.30	7.05	6.85	6.65	6.45	6.25	6.10	5.95	5.80	5.70	5.65
17 - 20	8.25	7.90	7.60	7.35	7.15	6.95	6.75	6.55	6.40	6.25	6.10	6.00	5.95
14 - 17	8.75	8.40	8.10	7.85	7.65	7.45	7.25	7.05	6.90	6.75	6.60	6.50	6.40
11 - 14	9.45	9.10	8.80	8.55	8.30	8.05	7.85	7.65	7.45	7.30	7.15	7.05	6.95
8 - 11	10.35	10.00	9.70	9.45	9.20	8.95	8.75	8.55	8.35	8.20	8.05	7.95	7.85
5 - 8%	11.25	10.90	10.60	10.35	10.10	9.85	9.65	9.45	9.25	9.10	8.95	8.85	8.75
	5 - 8%	8 - 11	11 - 14	14 - 17	17 - 20	20 - 23	23 - 26	26 - 29	29 - 32	32 - 35	35 - 38	38 - 41	41 - 44

CORN'S ESTIMATED CARRYOVER AS % OF TOTAL USE

SOYBEAN'S LOW PROTECTIVE PRICE — UNDER AVERAGE CONDITIONS

SOYBEAN'S ESTIMATED CARRYOVER AS %													
23 - 26	$5.20	$5.15	$5.10	$5.05	$5.00	$4.95	$4.90	$4.85	$4.80	$4.75	$4.70	$4.65	$4.65
20 - 23	5.30	5.25	5.20	5.15	5.10	5.05	5.00	4.95	4.90	4.85	4.80	4.75	4.70
17 - 20	5.50	5.40	5.30	5.25	5.20	5.15	5.10	5.05	5.00	4.95	4.90	4.85	4.80
14 - 17	5.65	5.55	5.45	5.40	5.35	5.30	5.25	5.20	5.15	5.10	5.05	5.00	4.95
11 - 14	5.90	5.80	5.70	5.60	5.55	5.50	5.45	5.40	5.35	5.30	5.25	5.20	5.15
8 - 11	6.20	6.10	6.00	5.90	5.85	5.80	5.75	5.70	5.65	5.60	5.55	5.50	5.45
5 - 8%	6.60	6.50	6.40	6.30	6.20	6.15	6.10	6.05	6.00	5.95	5.90	5.85	5.80
	5 - 8%	8 - 11	11 - 14	14 - 17	17 - 20	20 - 23	23 - 26	26 - 29	29 - 32	32 - 35	35 - 38	38 - 41	41 - 44

CORN'S ESTIMATED CARRYOVER AS % OF TOTAL USE

BUYING SOYBEANS
USE THE TABLES ON THIS PAGE WHEN CONDITIONS ARE POOR FOR A RISE IN SOYBEAN PRICES

AN EXAMPLE using these tables —

1. Let's suppose the points from the indicator page totaled -22. Therefore the "under poor conditions" tables are used.
2. Let's suppose the estimated soybean carryover at the end of the crop year next Aug. 31st is 15%.
3. Let's suppose the estimated carryover for corn at the end of the corn crop year next Sep. 30th is 36%.
4. Using those percentages on the top table, we get an estimated highest soybean price for the crop year of $6.40.
5. Using the bottom table, you get an estimated low protective price of $4.85.
6. Let's suppose that you had bought soybeans at $5.55. Then you will need $3500 as back-up capital in addition to the margin, and you can expect a profit of about $4250 in this example.

SOYBEAN'S ESTIMATED HIGHEST PRICE TABLES
— nearest month — UNDER POOR CONDITIONS

SOYBEAN'S ESTIMATED CARRYOVER AS %

	5 - 8%	8 - 11	11 - 14	14 - 17	17 - 20	20 - 23	23 - 26	26 - 29	29 - 32	32 - 35	35 - 38	38 - 41	41 - 44
23 - 26	$7.40	$7.10	$6.85	$6.60	$6.40	$6.20	$6.05	$5.90	$5.75	$5.65	$5.55	$5.45	$5.35
20 - 23	7.50	7.25	7.00	6.80	6.60	6.40	6.25	6.15	6.00	5.90	5.80	5.70	5.60
17 - 20	7.70	7.45	7.20	7.00	6.80	6.65	6.50	6.40	6.30	6.20	6.10	6.00	5.90
14 - 17	7.90	7.65	7.45	7.25	7.05	6.90	6.75	6.65	6.55	6.45	6.40	6.35	6.30
11 - 14	8.25	8.00	7.80	7.60	7.45	7.30	7.20	7.10	7.00	6.95	6.90	6.85	6.80
8 - 11	8.70	8.50	8.30	8.10	7.95	7.85	7.75	7.65	7.60	7.55	7.50	7.45	7.40
5 - 8%	9.35	9.15	8.95	8.80	8.65	8.55	8.45	8.35	8.30	8.25	8.20	8.15	8.10

CORN'S ESTIMATED CARRYOVER AS % OF TOTAL USE

SOYBEAN'S LOW PROTECTIVE PRICE — UNDER POOR CONDITIONS

SOYBEAN'S ESTIMATED CARRYOVER AS %

	5 - 8%	8 - 11	11 - 14	14 - 17	17 - 20	20 - 23	23 - 26	26 - 29	29 - 32	32 - 35	35 - 38	38 - 41	41 - 44
23 - 26	$5.00	$4.90	$4.80	$4.75	$4.70	$4.65	$4.60	$4.55	$4.50	$4.45	$4.40	$4.35	$4.30
20 - 23	5.10	5.00	4.90	4.85	4.80	4.75	4.70	4.65	4.60	4.55	4.50	4.45	4.40
17 - 20	5.25	5.15	5.05	5.00	4.95	4.90	4.85	4.80	4.75	4.70	4.65	4.60	4.55
14 - 17	5.45	5.35	5.25	5.20	5.15	5.10	5.05	5.00	4.95	4.90	4.85	4.80	4.75
11 - 14	5.65	5.55	5.45	5.40	5.35	5.30	5.25	5.20	5.15	5.10	5.05	5.00	4.95
8 - 11	5.90	5.80	5.75	5.70	5.65	5.60	5.55	5.50	5.45	5.40	5.35	5.30	5.25
5 - 8%	6.20	6.15	6.10	6.05	6.00	5.95	5.90	5.85	5.80	5.75	5.70	5.65	5.60

CORN'S ESTIMATED CARRYOVER AS % OF TOTAL USE

PART 2
SECTION A
BUYING SOYBEANS
using supply and demand data

In Part 1 you used the relationship between corn and soybeans to give an estimated highest price for the crop year. Here, in Part 2, you will again be finding the highest price but from a different set of data. In this section you will be using supply, total use, and the carryover as the basis for forecasting the highest price. (The lowest price will be dealt with in section B.)

There are three basic concepts behind the structure of the tables in this section. **The first concept** — stated briefly, it is this, "The year end carryover, expressed as % of total use, is a good indicator the sufficiency of the soybean supply for the crop year." Now for the explanation. A large soybean supply can be indicated in 3 different ways; (1) by a number, such as a total supply of 2.5 billion bu. would be a large supply (2) by a carryover, such as a year end carryover of 400 million bu. would suggest a large supply (3) by a carryover which is expressed **as % of total use** (carryover divided by the total use × 100 = % carryover). For example, an estimated 20% carryover would indicate a large supply of soybeans for that crop year.

This book will use the "carryover as % of total use" as the indicator of whether the supply of beans is tight or large. Thus, a 10% carryover or less would indicate a tight supply; whereas a 16% or more would suggest a large supply. The average of the past 6 years is a 13.6% carryover.

The concept restated says this — the size of the carryover, as % of total use, should indicate the potential for a price rise. For example, a carryover of 8% would indicate the potential for a good rise in prices because it shows a tight soybean supply; whereas an 18% carryover would indicate a limited price rise because supplies are large.

The second concept — This refers to the size of the initial price at the time you buy a soybean contract.

Think on this situation — at harvest time when prices are usually at their lowest, you consider buying July beans. The estimated carryover is 14%, an average size. You are figuring on July prices to rise. Here's the question — which of these two situations would likely give you the most profit: (1) if you bought the July soybeans at $6.50 (2) or, if you bought the July soybeans at $8.00? Which is likely to give you the most profit? Answer — the contract at $6.50. Why? Because the top price for this particular example with a 14% carryover will be near $8.00 — so there is lots of room for a price increase from

$6.50. Whereas, by buying at $8.00, there is little if any upside scope remaining — the price was too high to start with.

The concept will be reinstated — All other things being equal, buying soybeans at a low price will likely result in a better profit than buying at a high price. In other words, the price size influences profits. The same can be said when you go short soybeans — all other things being equal, the higher the price when you sell soybeans, the more profit you are likely to make.

The third concept — The economy, as it affects soybean prices, is taken into account by using the soybean economic indicators for Part 1. The results of the economic indicators will be used by three sets of price tables — one for poor soybean price conditions, one for average soybean price conditions, and one for good soybean price conditions.

Please look at the following three price tables. These are the tables to use when you are intending to buy soybeans. By the way, most of the buying of soybeans is done at harvest time when prices are generally at their lowest — and the July contract is usually bought because the peak price usually occurs in the late spring or early summer. You will note that one table is for good soybean price conditions, one for average, and one for poor conditions. Look at the bottom row. The prices here are the lowest closing price — it is assumed you are trying to buy in at the lowest price. Look at the sides, and you will see the % carryover. Note that they go by even numbers. i.e. 12%, 14% etc. You will likely need to interpolate to obtain the highest price estimate. The following example will show you how to use the tables.

Example — the time is in the fall. You think you would like to buy July soybeans.

1. The most recent USDA crop report provides data which indicate an estimated carryover for the end of the crop year next Aug. 31st will be 14%.

2. Using the economic indicators in Part 1, you find that they indicate an average condition for soybean price possibilities. You turn to the table which says, "- under average conditions".

3. You believe prices have bottomed out for the harvest season, so you are ready to buy a July contract. Look for the lowest closing price of the **July contract.** Let's assume it was $6.25. Don't worry if you don't get the correct lowest close price to start with. You can adjust the objective price later. At this point, all you want to know is this, "Is there enough profit potential to make the trade worthwhile?" If there isn't, then you can trade some other commodity. The most difficult thing, though, is to know when to buy July soybeans. It is not easy to get in near the bottom, but only you can make that decision.

4. Use the 14% carryover, the $6.25 July contract low price, and the "average conditions" tables. You obtain $8.10 as the estimated price objective for the July contract. It show a good potential profit.

5. Now you will need to know **when** to get out of the trade: in other words, you want to know when that top price will likely occur. That comes under "Timing". Part 3 will deal with timing.

Another Example - Follow this in the tables. You will need to interpolate to find this answer.

1. You will buy July soybeans. From the latest USDA report, you estimate the carryover to be 12.5%.

2. The lowest closing price for the July soybeans was $6.40.

3. The soybean economic indicators show that conditions are **good** for a price rise.

4. Using the table "under Good conditions", and using 12.5%, and using $6.40 — you will get $9.14 as the estimated July price objective.

5. From Part 3, you will find the time frame when that highest price will likely occur.

Remember that soybean futures are volatile and will sometimes change trend for no apparent reason. These tables are a guide only, and are an effort to apply soybean fundamentals in a reasonable approach to pricing and timing. It is good practice to review the economic indicators and the price objective every month or two because some factor may come into the market which will alter your previous forecast.

Buying Soybeans — under GOOD conditions
ESTIMATED PRICE OBJECTIVE

SOYBEAN CARRYOVER — AS % OF TOTAL USE

CARRYOVER	$4.75	$5.00	$5.25	$5.50	$5.75	$6.00	$6.25	$6.50	$6.75	$7.00	$7.25	$7.50	$7.75	$8.00	$8.25
22%	6.50	6.65	6.80	6.90	7.00	7.10	7.20	7.30	7.40	7.50	7.60	7.70			
20%	6.70	6.85	7.00	7.15	7.30	7.45	7.60	7.70	7.80	7.90	8.00	8.10	8.20	8.30	
18%	7.05	7.20	7.35	7.50	7.65	7.80	7.95	8.10	8.20	8.30	8.40	8.50	8.60	8.70	8.75
16%	7.50	7.65	7.80	7.95	8.10	8.20	8.30	8.40	8.50	8.60	8.70	8.80	8.90	9.00	9.10
14%	8.10	8.25	8.40	8.50	8.60	8.70	8.80	8.90	9.00	9.10	9.20	9.30	9.40	9.45	9.50
12%	8.65	8.75	8.80	8.85	8.90	9.00	9.15	9.30	9.40	9.50	9.60	9.70	9.75	9.80	9.85
10%	9.00	9.10	9.15	9.20	9.25	9.35	9.45	9.60	9.70	9.80	9.90	9.95	10.00	10.05	10.10
8%	9.30	9.40	9.50	9.60	9.70	9.80	9.90	10.00	10.10	10.20	10.30	10.35	10.40	10.45	10.50
6%	9.50	9.65	9.80	10.00	10.20	10.35	10.50	10.65	10.75	10.85	10.90	10.95	11.00	11.05	11.10
	$4.75	$5.00	$5.25	$5.50	$5.75	$6.00	$6.25	$6.50	$6.75	$7.00	$7.25	$7.50	$7.75	$8.00	$8.25

SOYBEAN'S LOWEST CLOSING PRICE OF THE CONTRACT MONTH BEING DETERMINED

15

Buying Soybeans — under AVERAGE conditions
ESTIMATED PRICE OBJECTIVE

Do not buy Soybeans here. There is little or no upside potential in this area.

SOYBEAN CARRYOVER — AS % OF TOTAL USE	$4.75	$5.00	$5.25	$5.50	$5.75	$6.00	$6.25	$6.50	$6.75	$7.00	$7.25	$7.50	$7.75	$8.00	$8.25	
22%	6.30	6.40	6.50	6.55	6.60	6.65	6.70	6.75								22%
20%	6.45	6.60	6.70	6.80	6.90	6.95	7.00	7.05	7.10							20%
18%	6.65	6.80	6.90	7.00	7.10	7.20	7.30	7.35	7.40	7.45	7.50					18%
16%	7.00	7.15	7.25	7.35	7.45	7.55	7.60	7.65	7.70	7.75	7.80	7.85				16%
14%	7.45	7.60	7.70	7.80	7.90	8.00	8.10	8.15	8.20	8.25	8.30	8.35	8.40	8.45		14%
12%	7.90	8.00	8.10	8.20	8.30	8.40	8.50	8.60	8.65	8.70	8.75	8.80	8.85	8.90	8.95	12%
10%	8.25	8.35	8.45	8.55	8.65	8.75	8.85	8.95	9.00	9.05	9.10	9.15	9.20	9.25	9.30	10%
8%	8.60	8.70	8.80	8.90	9.00	9.10	9.20	9.30	9.40	9.50	9.55	9.60	9.65	9.70	9.75	8%
6%	8.90	9.00	9.10	9.20	9.30	9.40	9.50	9.60	9.70	9.80	9.90	10.00	10.10	10.20	10.25	6%
	$4.75	$5.00	$5.25	$5.50	$5.75	$6.00	$6.25	$6.50	$6.75	$7.00	$7.25	$7.50	$7.75	$8.00	$8.25	

SOYBEAN'S LOWEST CLOSING PRICE OF THE CONTRACT MONTH BEING DETERMINED

16

Buying Soybeans — under POOR conditions
ESTIMATED PRICE OBJECTIVE

SOYBEAN CARRYOVER — AS % OF TOTAL USE

Carryover	$4.75	$5.00	$5.25	$5.50	$5.75	$6.00	$6.25	$6.50	$6.75	$7.00	$7.25	$7.50	$7.75	$8.00	$8.25
22%	5.55	5.70	5.80	5.90	6.00										
20%	5.65	5.80	5.90	6.00	6.10	6.20									
18%	5.85	6.00	6.15	6.30	6.40	6.45	6.50								
16%	6.05	6.20	6.35	6.45	6.55	6.60	6.65	6.70							
14%	6.30	6.45	6.60	6.70	6.80	6.90	7.00	7.10	7.15	7.20					
12%	6.70	6.85	7.00	7.15	7.30	7.40	7.50	7.60	7.65	7.70	7.75	7.80			
10%	7.20	7.35	7.45	7.55	7.65	7.75	7.85	7.90	7.95	8.00	8.05	8.10	8.15	8.20	
8%	7.80	7.95	8.05	8.15	8.25	8.35	8.40	8.45	8.50	8.55	8.60	8.65	8.70	8.75	8.80
6%	8.50	8.65	8.80	8.90	9.00	9.10	9.20	9.25	9.30	9.35	9.40	9.45	9.50	9.55	9.60

Do not buy Soybeans here. There is little or no upside potential in this area.

SOYBEAN'S LOWEST CLOSING PRICE OF THE CONTRACT MONTH BEING DETERMINED

SECTION B
SELLING SOYBEANS

Usually the highest soybean price occurs in the late spring or summer, and the lowest price usually bottoms out in the fall, at or near harvest. For that reason, when one sells a soybean contract, he usually chooses the November contract. The position is most often taken in June to August, and most often liquidated from Sept. to the end of November.

To use the following tables, you will need to know the following:

1. You need to know the estimated % carryover. You should recalculate it from the most recent USDA data which is likely different from the data used when you previously bought soybeans about 6 or 7 months previously. It is likely more accurate.

2. You need to know the highest price for the contract month you are going to find. Naturally the best time to sell beans is after the price has peaked — and it is difficult to know when that has happened, but only you can make that decision. Most people will be selling the November contract because they expect the lowest price at harvest.

3. You need to know from the soybean economic indicators whether you should be using the table for "good conditions", or for "average conditions", or for "poor conditions". Then select the appropriate table. The economic indicators will likely be completely different from the time you used them to buy beans about seven months previously.

Example — selling November soybeans.

The situation — the time is mid-July — the peak price seems to have occurred, giving the Nov. highest price as $8.50 — the economic indicators point to "average conditions" for soybean prices — the latest USDA report provides information which indicates a carryover of 12 % of total use.

The action — (1) Turn to the table which says, "Selling Soybeans under average conditions". (2) Using 12% carryover and $8.50 for the highest November price, you get $6.90 as the estimated price objective for selling November beans — a potential profit of $8000. (3) This example needed no interpolation. But in real life, nearly all estimates will require interpolation. (4) You will want to know when to take your profits. That comes under "timing" which is in Part 3.

SELLING SOYBEANS — under GOOD conditions
ESTIMATED PRICE OBJECTIVE

SOYBEAN'S HIGHEST CLOSING PRICE	22%	20%	18%	16%	14%	12%	10%	8%	6%
13.50	6.90	7.10	7.35	7.75	8.30	8.85	9.45	10.05	10.70
13.00	6.85	7.05	7.25	7.65	8.20	8.75	9.35	9.90	10.50
12.50	6.80	6.95	7.15	7.55	8.10	8.65	9.20	9.75	10.30
12.00	6.70	6.85	7.05	7.45	7.95	8.50	9.05	9.55	10.10
11.50	6.60	6.75	6.95	7.30	7.80	8.35	8.90	9.35	9.90
11.00	6.50	6.65	6.85	7.15	7.65	8.20	8.70	9.15	9.70
10.50	6.40	6.55	6.75	7.00	7.50	8.05	8.50	8.95	9.50
10.00	6.35	6.45	6.60	6.85	7.35	7.85	8.25	8.75	9.30
9.50	6.20	6.30	6.45	6.70	7.15	7.65	8.00	8.50	9.00
9.00	6.00	6.10	6.25	6.50	6.90	7.35	7.70	8.20	8.70
8.50	5.70	5.80	6.00	6.25	6.60	7.00	7.35	7.85	8.30
8.00	5.55	5.60	5.80	6.00	6.30	6.70	7.05	7.50	8.00
7.50	5.35	5.40	5.60	5.80	6.05	6.40	6.75	7.20	7.70
7.00	5.15	5.20	5.40	5.60	5.85	6.15	6.50	6.95	7.50
6.50	5.05	5.10	5.20	5.40	5.65	5.95	6.35	6.80	7.40

SOYBEAN'S HIGHEST CLOSING PRICE — FOR THE CONTRACT MONTH BEING DETERMINED

ESTIMATED SOYBEAN CARRYOVER — AS % OF TOTAL USE

SELLING SOYBEANS — under AVERAGE conditions
ESTIMATED PRICE OBJECTIVE

SOYBEAN'S HIGHEST CLOSING PRICE — FOR THE CONTRACT MONTH BEING DETERMINED

	6.50	6.75	7.00	7.25	7.50	7.75	8.00	8.25	8.50	8.75	9.00	9.25	9.50	9.75	10.00
22%	5.00	5.05	5.10	5.15	5.25	5.35	5.50	5.60	5.70	5.80	5.90	6.00	6.15	6.30	6.45
20%	5.10	5.15	5.20	5.30	5.40	5.50	5.60	5.70	5.80	5.90	6.00	6.15	6.30	6.45	6.60
18%	5.20	5.30	5.40	5.50	5.60	5.70	5.80	5.90	6.00	6.10	6.20	6.35	6.50	6.65	6.80
16%	5.30	5.40	5.50	5.60	5.70	5.80	5.90	6.05	6.20	6.35	6.50	6.65	6.85	7.05	7.25
14%	5.50	5.60	5.70	5.80	5.90	6.00	6.15	6.30	6.50	6.70	6.90	7.10	7.30	7.50	7.75
12%	5.70	5.80	5.95	6.10	6.25	6.40	6.55	6.70	6.90	7.10	7.30	7.50	7.70	7.90	8.05
10%	6.00	6.10	6.25	6.40	6.55	6.70	6.85	7.00	7.20	7.40	7.60	7.80	8.00	8.20	8.35
8%	6.30	6.40	6.55	6.70	6.85	7.00	7.20	7.40	7.60	7.80	8.00	8.20	8.40	8.55	8.70
6%	6.70	6.80	6.90	7.05	7.20	7.40	7.55	7.75	8.00	8.20	8.40	8.60	8.75	8.90	9.05

ESTIMATED SOYBEAN CARRYOVER — AS % OF TOTAL USE

SELLING SOYBEANS — under POOR conditions
ESTIMATED PRICE OBJECTIVE

Highest Closing Price	22%	20%	18%	16%	14%	12%	10%	8%	6%	
9.25	5.70	5.95	6.20	6.50	6.80	7.15	7.55	8.00	8.50	9.25
9.00	5.60	5.80	6.00	6.35	6.65	7.00	7.40	7.80	8.25	9.00
8.75	5.50	5.65	5.85	6.15	6.45	6.80	7.15	7.55	8.00	8.75
8.50	5.40	5.50	5.70	5.60	6.25	6.60	6.95	7.35	7.80	8.50
8.25	5.30	5.40	5.60	5.85	6.10	6.40	6.75	7.15	7.60	8.25
8.00	5.20	5.30	5.50	5.70	5.95	6.20	6.55	6.95	7.40	8.00
7.75	5.15	5.20	5.40	5.60	5.80	6.00	6.35	6.75	7.20	7.75
7.50	5.10	5.15	5.30	5.45	5.65	5.85	6.20	6.60	7.05	7.50
7.25	5.05	5.10	5.20	5.30	5.50	5.65	6.00	6.45	6.90	7.25
7.00	5.00	5.05	5.10	5.20	5.35	5.50	5.85	6.30	6.75	7.00
6.75	4.95	5.00	5.05	5.15	5.25	5.35	5.70	6.15	6.60	6.75
6.50	4.90	4.95	5.00	5.05	5.15	5.25	5.60	6.00	6.45	6.50
6.25	4.85	4.90	4.95	5.00	5.10	5.20	5.50	5.85	6.30	6.25
6.00	4.80	4.85	4.90	4.95	5.05	5.15	5.40	5.70	6.15	6.00
5.75	4.75	4.80	4.85	4.90	5.00	5.10	5.30	5.60	6.05	5.75
	22%	20%	18%	16%	14%	12%	10%	8%	6%	

ESTIMATED SOYBEAN CARRYOVER — AS % OF TOTAL USE

SOYBEAN'S HIGHEST CLOSING PRICE — FOR THE CONTRACT MONTH BEING DETERMINED

SOMETHING NEW IS ADDED

The selling of soybeans requires an additional, extra action which is not needed when you buy soybeans. That's because when you buy soybeans, it is usually in the fall and you liquidate in the late spring or summer. But when you sell soybeans, you will likely be liquidating them in the fall which is in the first part of the next crop year. Thus, there are two crop years involved when you sell November soybeans.

This presents a problem. When you first took the short position in beans (in July, for example), you used the % carryover at that time (12%, for example) to find the estimated price objective. But, as time passed, you found you were in the month of September which is the first month of the next crop year.

Now there is a new crop to contend with — which includes a new supply estimate and a new % carryover estimate. This new estimate of the % carryover for the new crop year can be quite different from the % carryover you have been using so far — and therefore it can alter your estimated price objective.

Refer back to the example of selling soybeans which was done a few paragraphs back. A 12% carryover was used to obtain a price objective of $6.90 from the table. Now suppose this happens. From the latest USDA data on the new crop about to be harvested, you calculate that the new carryover will be about 18%. That's big. It means there will be plenty of soybeans left over at the end of the next crop year. Such a change from 12% to 18% will alter the estimated $6.90 price objective — maybe even lowering it to $6.50, which could mean another $2000.

What to do? — That's where the table in Part 4 will be used. It will give you an estimated objective price adjustment factor to use. It will tell you how much you may have to change your objective price.

PART 3
TIMING
selecting the time frame for
SOYBEAN'S HIGHEST PRICE

The general rule for timing is this — the tighter the soybean supply, the sooner in the year prices will peak. (A tight supply is shown by the small carryover at the end of the crop year — expressed in bushels or as a % of total use.)

Just a reminder about carryover. Carryover can be expressed in bushels, e.g. 225 million bu. Or the carryover can be expressed as % of estimated total use for the crop year (total use is exports plus domestic use). The equation is; carryover divided by total use × 100 = carryover as %. The percent carryover gives a truer picture of the carryover actual size. For example, a 10% carryover means there is only a 36.5 day's supply of soybeans remaining at the end of the crop year (365 × 10%). The average of the past 6 years is 13.6%. This book uses the % carryover throughout.

The timing of soybean's highest price is difficult to pin down due to soybean's volatile trading pattern. But the following information will serve as a guide to a time frame in which one can reasonably expect the highest price to occur. The following information is based on the past performance of soybean prices. It is to serve as a guide only. The timing selection is based on the size of the carryover in %.

GUIDE TO THE TIMING OF SOYBEAN'S HIGHEST PRICE OF THE CROP YEAR

For a carryover of 5% to 8% — these percentage carryover numbers represent a very small supply of soybeans for the crop year. It means that the highest price will be much higher than average. It also means that the highest price will likely occur **between April 15th and June 1st,** with the smaller percentage number favoring the early part of the time frame.

For a carryover of 8% to 11% — these percentage carryover numbers represent a soybean supply which is smaller than average but not serious enough to cause prices to rise to record highs. The crop years with this size of carryover tend to peak **between May 15th and June 15th.**

For a carryover of 11% to 14% — this is an average size carryover which indicates an average size soybean supply. The highest prices for these crop years are likely to occur **from June 1st to July 15th.**

For a carryover of 14% to 17% — these carryover numbers represent a larger than average supply of beans. With such a large supply the highest price is not very high — but what there is of it will often occur **from July 1st to August 15th.**

For a carryover of 17% to 20% — with such a large carryover, prices are depressed and there is a chance there will not be a high price, just a flat price or a decline from the previous harvest price. But, if there is to be a highest price, it will likely occur late in the summer, often **from August 1st to October 1st.**

Keep in mind that the time frames above are certainly not 100% accurate. Soybeans are very volatile and unpredictable in nature. However, it is better to have a rough guide to the timing of the highest price than to have no guide at all.

SECTION B
selecting the time frame for
SOYBEAN'S LOWEST PRICE

Selecting the time frame for the lowest price is different from finding it for the highest price. There are a few general rules.
1. The low prices tend to occur from early fall to mid winter.
2. The years with a smaller % carryover tend to bottom out earlier than those with a large %.
3. Because the lowest price often occurs at harvest time which is the beginning of a new crop year, you will therefore have two % carryovers to take into account — the one of the crop year you are in, and the one for the new crop which is about to be harvested. To give you an idea of how the two carryovers work together, **follow this example.** Suppose the time is June and you have decided to sell Nov. soybeans because you think the peak price has already happened. Suppose the carryover for the year you are in is 10%, and suppose you learn from the monthly USDA crop report (ask your broker for it) that the carryover for the next crop year, the one about to be harvested, will have an estimated carryover of about 18%. So now you have two carryovers to contend with. The low 10% carryover of the year you are in will tend to bottom out early, whereas the larger 18% one will tend to be later. Past performances of soybean prices show that there will be a compromise between the two — but not a perfect compromise because the year you are in will continue to hold the dominant position. The end result should be something like this: the early date of the 10% carryover year will be delayed by about 2 or 3 weeks.

Please look at the following table, "The estimated time frame for the lowest price".

1. Look at the left side of the table and you will see, "Estimated carryover % **for the year you are in".**
2. Look at the top of the table where it says, "estimated carryover % **for the next crop year.".**

3. Note, also, that the % carryovers are grouped, e.g. 5% to 8%, 8% to 11%, etc.
Example: to illustrate how the table works, follow this example.

The setting — the date is July 1979. You believe the top price has been reached so you are thinking of going short Nov. soybeans (or Dec. meal or Dec. oil). You are going to use the table to find an estimated date or time frame when you think the price will be at its lowest. Thus, you will learn how long you might have to hold the position, and you will know when to be alerted to take your profit.

The data — The carryover for the crop year 1978/79 that you are in is 9%. The USDA crop report of July indicates an estimated carryover for the new crop coming up of 18%.

Using the table — 1. Look at the left side. Locate the group which will contain the 9% carryover (it is the 8% to 11% group). 2. On the top line, locate the group where the new carryover of 18% will be located (it is the 17% to 20% group). 3. Look across the table from the 9%, look down the table from the 18% and you will converge on the square where it says, "Oct. 15 to Dec. 1". That's when to expect the low price to occur.

Comment — that is a fairly large time frame, six weeks. But that's the way it is with soybeans which are volatile and unpredictable. However, you may try to narrow it down by asking yourself, "Is the low price more likely to occur in the first half of the time frame, than in the second half?" A reasonable answer will be "yes" because you are using a 9% carryover which is a small number which tends to bottom out earlier than average. And "the year you are in" is more dominant than "the next crop year". (This example was an actual trade — and the low price for the trade occured on Oct. 29, 1979).

The Estimated Time Frame for the Lowest Price

ESTIMATED CARRYOVER % FOR THE CROP YEAR YOU ARE IN

	ESTIMATED CARRYOVER % FOR THE NEXT CROP YEAR				
	5% to 8%	8% to 11%	11% to 14%	14% to 17%	17% to 20%
5% to 8%	Sept. 1 to Oct. 1	Sept. 1 to Oct. 15	Sept. 15 to Nov. 1	Oct. 1 to Nov. 15	Oct. 15 to Dec. 1
8% to 11%	Sept. 15 to Oct. 15	Sept. 15 to Nov. 1	Oct. 1 to Nov. 1	Oct. 1 to Nov. 15	Oct. 15 to Dec. 1
11% to 14%	Sept. 15 to Nov. 1	Oct. 1 to Nov. 1	Oct. 1 to Nov. 15	Oct. 15 to Dec. 1	Nov. 1 to Dec. 15
14% to 17%	Oct. 1 to Nov. 15	Oct. 1 to Dec. 1	Oct. 15 to Dec. 1	Nov. 1 to Dec. 15	Nov. 15 to Dec. 15
17% to 20%	Oct. 15 to Dec. 1	Oct. 15 to Dec. 1	Nov. 1 to Dec. 15	Nov. 15 to Dec. 31	Dec. 1 to Dec. 31

PART 4
SECTION A
SELLING NOV. OR JAN. SOYBEANS

How will the carryover of the next soybean crop affect the low price objective?

The highest price of the crop year usually occurs in the late spring or summer. The lowest price usually occurs from October to December. Therefore, when one wishes to go short in soybeans, he will likely take the position in the late spring or summer, and take his profits in the fall or early winter. That means that the logical contract to sell would be the November or January soybean futures contract.

When the short position is first taken, the trader or hedger would know only of the carryover for the year he was in. For example, when he sold Nov. beans in the spring, he knew that the carryover was 13%, as an example, Using the tables in Part 2, he would find his lowest price objective when he intended to liquidate the contract.

But, as July and August pass in time, he is now aware of the next crop's size and its estimate carryover. That maturing crop will begin to be harvested in September. He will obtain the carryover % estimate from USDA data released in July. About this time, the market is being influenced by the new crop's size. Therefore, the trader or hedger should adjust his original lowest price estimated objective — and the following table will help him do that very thing.

An adjustment will be particularly important if there is a large difference in the estimated carryovers. **For example,** A carryover of 13% in the present year, and an expected carryover of 14% in the next year would cause almost no change in the low price objective. But, if the present carryover was 10%, and the next crop's carryover was 17%, then an adjustment is necessary — in this case, the low expected price would fall lower than originally indicated, much lower.

Another example — Suppose your present carryover was 15% and the next year's carryover is estimated at only 8%. This means that next year's crop is much smaller, therefore it is bullish. In this case the original low price objective would have to be adjusted upward. That's where the following table comes in.

Please look at the following table, "Selling Soybeans — Nov. or Jan. contract". Note the % column down the middle — that is the % carryover for the year you are in when you took the short Nov. beans contract. Note the % differences across the top, ranging from +7% to -7%. They are the % differences of the next crop year.

Here is an example of what is meant by the statement above. Suppose the carryover for the present crop year is 10% when you take the short position in June, for example. In

July, you learn from USDA data that the estimated carryover for the coming new crop year will be 16%. That is a +6% carryover difference — the numbers along the top row. Therefore, you will use the adjustment numbers in the +6% column.

Another example — the present carryover is 14%, the next carryover is estimated at 11%. That is a -3% carryover difference — so the numbers in the -3% column will be used.

Look at the numbers in the body of the table. They are in %, e.g. -6%, -2%, 0%, +4% etc. They are the adjustments which will be applied to the low price objective obtained from the tables in Part 2. It is now time for a complete example of their use.

Example — In June you decided to sell November soybeans because you believed bean prices had peaked. (Follow this example in the table for practice). The economic indicators show an average year, the carryover is 12% for the year you are in, the highest Nov. soybean price was $8.00.

Using the "Selling Soybeans — under Average conditions" table in Part 2, you see the lowest price objective is $6.55. In July, from USDA crop data you estimate the carryover for the next crop which is about to be harvested, to be 8%, which is a change of -4%.

In the table, find 12% in the "Present Carryover" column, in the middle. Look to the right under the -4% heading and you will see +9% as the adjustment factor. That +9% will be multiplied by the original price objective of $6.55, then added to the $6.55. Here is the calculation: $6.55 × 9% = 59¢, $6.55 + 59¢ = $7.14. The new, adjusted low price objective is $7.14. (Note that it was the original price objective from the table in Part 2 which was multiplied by the adjustment % factor.)

Another example — You went short Nov. soybeans using the Nov. highest price of $7.50, a carryover of 14%, average economic conditions. From the appropriate table you obtained $5.90 as the low price objective where you will take your profit.

In July, you use USDA data to find the carryover for the crop year coming up — which is a large crop with an 18% estimated carryover, a change of +4%. Find 14% in the center column "Present Carryover". Look to the left under the heading +4% column, and you will get -5% as the adjustment factor. Using the original objective of $5.90, we do the following calculation: $5.90 × 5% = 30¢, $5.90 - 30¢ = $5.60. The new adjusted price objective is $5.60. You will have already found the time frame for the lowest price from Part 3.

IMPORTANT — read this. The question may have come to you, "Should I hold my short position until the price objective has been reached?" The answer is this: the prices from the tables are estimates only, estimates based on past price experience and an equation. Because they are estimates, they are to be considered a guide, an opinion. Because they are estimates, the prices may be right on, but more likely they will differ from the real, final lowest or highest price by an X number of cents.

The decision to take a position, and the decision to liquidate that position can be done only by you. You, and only you, can make those important decisions — and they are not easy to make. But you can use some good aids. The common ones are such things as moving averages, RSI, bullish consensus to name a few. Now there is this book with its helpful tables. But the final decision depends on you.

SECTION B
RATING THE SOYBEAN PROFIT OPPORTUNITIES

When it comes to selling a soybean contract, it is wise to check the tables to see whether it is worthwhile to do. Profit opportunities vary. There are some trades where one can expect a drop of $2.00, ($10,000) from the highest price, and there are some which may show only a 25¢ decline. A small decline like 25¢ is not worth the risk because soybean prices are volatile and can change 20¢ quickly, for no apparent reason.

Here is an example of a good profit opportunity. The present carryover is 7%, the next crop year's carryover is estimated at 18%. That means the following: a 7% carryover represents a small supply which could have a high Nov. price, likely near $9.00. The 18% carryover for the crop coming up tells us that the crop is big, which could cause prices to fall as low as $6.50. This example shows a good profit.

Here is an example where one should not sell soybeans at all. Present carryover is 16%, the carryover for the next crop year is estimated at 7%. A 16% carryover means a large supply of soybeans, so the highest price was likely not very high. Then comes a tight supply (7%). As a result, bean prices are liable to rise right through to next Spring — not coming down at harvest at all.

Look at the following table. Look at the left side. This is where the present carryover is located. Look at the top row — that is the estimated carryover for the next crop year. Inside the squares you will see the rating of the profit opportunities — such words as, "The Best, Good, Average, ?, Poor". The ? indicates a risky area with a small potential profit which could swing one way or the other. The word "Poor" indicates almost no chance for profit.

Example — Present carryover is 12%, next crop carryover is estimated at 17%. The square where they intersect is "Good". There should be a good profit in this trade.

SELLING SOYBEANS — Nov. or Jan. Contract

ESTIMATED % CARRYOVER DIFFERENCE OF THE NEXT CROP YEAR

+7%	+6%	+5%	+4%	+3%	+2%	+1%	0%	Present Carryover	-1%	-2%	-3%	-4%	-5%	-6%	-7%
-6	-5	-4	-3	-2	0			6%							
-7	-6	-5	-3	-2	-1	0		7%							
-7	-6	-5	-4	-2	-1	0	0	8%	+4						
-8	-7	-6	-4	-3	-2	-1	0	9%	+4	+7					
-8	-7	-6	-4	-3	-2	-1	0	10%	+3	+6	+9				
-9	-7	-6	-4	-3	-2	-1	0	11%	+3	+5	+8	+10			
-9	-8	-6	-5	-3	-2	-1	-1	12%	+3	+4	+6	+9	+10		
-10	-8	-7	-5	-4	-3	-2	-1	13%	+2	+4	+6	+8	+10	+12	
	-8	-7	-5	-4	-3	-2	-1	14%	+2	+4	+6	+8	+10	+12	+14
		-7	-5	-4	-3	-2	-2	15%	+1	+3	+5	+7	+9	+11	+13
			-5	-4	-3	-2	-2	16%	+1	+3	+5	+7	+9	+10	+12
				-5	-4	-3	-2	17%	0	+2	+4	+6	+8	+9	+11
					-4	-3	-2	18%	0	+2	+4	+6	+8	+9	+11
						-3	-3	19%	0	+1	+3	+5	+7	+8	+10
							-3	20%	0	+1	+3	+5	+6	+7	+9
								21%	0	0	+2	+4	+5	+6	+8
								22%	0	0	+2	+3	+4	+6	+7

DO NOT SELL SOYBEANS HERE. THERE IS NO DOWNSIDE POTENTIAL IN THIS AREA.

THE LOAN RATE WILL SUPPORT PRICES HERE

30

Selling Soybeans — November or January contract

RATING THE PROFIT OPPORTUNITIES

THE ESTIMATED CARRYOVER % FOR THE NEXT CROP YEAR

	5% to 8%	8% to 11%	11% to 14%	14% to 17%	17% to 20%	20% to 23%
5% to 8%	?	?	AVERAGE	GOOD	THE BEST	THE BEST
8% to 11%	?	?	AVERAGE	GOOD	GOOD	THE BEST
11% to 14%	POOR	?	AVERAGE	AVERAGE	GOOD	GOOD
14% to 17%	POOR	?	?	AVERAGE	AVERAGE	AVERAGE
17% to 20%	POOR	POOR	?	?	?	?
20% to 23%	POOR	POOR	POOR	POOR	?	?

THE ESTIMATED CARRYOVER % OF THE YEAR YOU ARE IN

PART 5
WHICH IS THE BEST TRADE
SOYBEANS?
SOYBEAN MEAL?
SOYBEAN OIL?

There are times when you can earn more money, per dollar invested, by trading in soybean meal only, rather that in soybeans themselves. And sometimes it is soybean oil which will present the most profitable opportunity. Then, again, sometimes it is soybeans themselves which offer the best advantange. It is always the best policy to trade in the soybean product which will give you the best percentage of profit on the amount of money being used in the trade. We speak of "percentage profit" here because the amount of money needed for a meal trade is less than needed for a soybean trade, for example, but the "percent profit" may be larger on the meal.

The graph in this section is designed to give you a quick answer to the question, "Should I trade in soybeans themselves or in one of its product in order to obtain the best percentage profit?"

Follow these examples on the graph.

Example 1. If soybean oil is 28¢ when soybeans are $7.00, which would be the best one to trade? Answer: move vertically on the $7.00 column, and hoizontally along the 28¢ line. The two lines converge in the area which says, "trade soybean oil only in this area". Therefore, one could figure on making a better return on his capital by trading in soybean oil rather than in meal or beans.

Example 2: if soybean oil is 24¢ and soybeans are $7.00, which trade is best? Answer: it would be best to trade soybeans because this is a neutral area between oil and meal where their profit potential are about the same. Therefore, soybeans would be a safer trade.

Example 3: if soybean oil is 26.3¢ and soybeans are $8.75, which is the best trade? Answer: soybean meal.

STRATEGY

Rule: The farther the convergence point moves deeper into the area of one of the products and away from the neutral area, the more profitable it becomes. To illustrate, follow these on the graph:

(a) oil at 23¢, Beans at $6.00 — a borderline case, not definite.

(b) oil at 26¢, beans at $6.50 — it is more profitable to trade in soybean oil.

(c) oil at 31¢, beans at $7.00 — oil has become even more profitable.

Rule: But when the point of convergence begins to move back, closer to the neutral area, it means that the prime profitable position is beginning to slip away. That is when one must consider changing to a soybean position or into the other product. To illustrate this point, the example above will be continued. Follow it on the graph.

(d) oil at 32¢, beans at $8.00. The convergence point has moved closer to the neutral area so it is time to consider switching to beans or meal. Check the situation daily because oil may move back out a bit.

(e) oil at 33¢, beans at $8.75. This is likely where one's suspicians are confirmed. It is likely wiser to switch to beans or meal.

But which trade — beans or meal? A trade in soybeans would be safer because, in effect, when you have a position in soybeans you actually have a position in both oil and meal simultaneously. Therefore, this would be a safer trade in case oil's convergence point changed direction and moved farther away from the neutral zone instead of into the neutral area. On the other hand (and only you can make this kind of decision) a position in soybean meal would be more profitable percentagewise, provided oil kept moving into the neutral area. Why? Because the bullish soybean oil price had taken a greater share of the bean price, leaving the meal with a smaller share; therefore, when oil begins to give up some of its portion of the soybean price (as shown by the convergence point moving closer to the neutral area), the meal is the one which benefits by that amount. In other words, when one product decreases in value, the other product increases in value.

BEST TRADING AREAS FOR SOYBEANS, SOYBEAN OIL, SOYBEAN MEAL

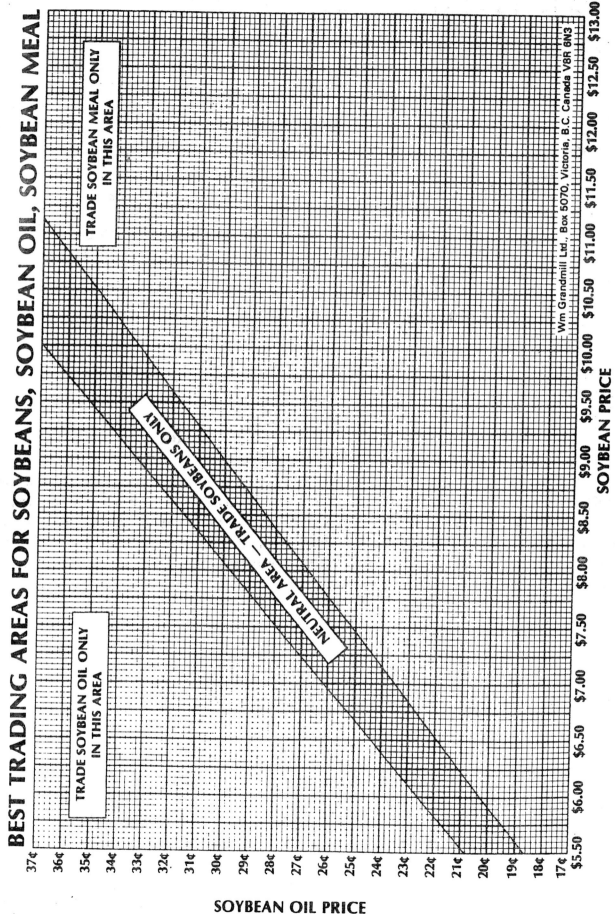

TRADE SOYBEAN MEAL ONLY IN THIS AREA

TRADE SOYBEAN OIL ONLY IN THIS AREA

NEUTRAL AREA — TRADE SOYBEANS ONLY

SOYBEAN PRICE

SOYBEAN OIL PRICE

Wm Grandmill Ltd., Box 5070, Victoria, B.C. Canada V8R 6N3

34

PART 6
SECTION A
TO FIND THE ESTIMATED
SOYBEAN MEAL PRICE

The following two tables are designed to find the estimated soybean meal price by using the **soybean price** and the **soybean oil price** together.

The tables have a crushing cost built into them of 28.5¢ per bushel. The 28.5¢ was considered to be the average crush margin over the past 5 years.

However, because the 28.5¢ is the **average** crushing cost or crush margin as it shall be called here, then we can assume that sometimes the crush margin will be more than 28.5¢, and sometimes less. That means that the prices for soybean meal from the tables are estimated correct for a 28.5¢ crush margin, but the prices could vary by a dollar or so if the crush margin was much different. Just to give you an idea how the various crush margins can affect meal prices, a crush margin of 26¢ would lower the price from the tables by $1., and a crush margin of 31¢ would raise the price from the tables by $1.

But, because most traders don't know what the crush margin is at the time they take their trade in meal or oil, it is best to use the tables just as they are. Another point: the crush margin tends to be more than 28.5¢ when soybean supplies are tight, whereas the crush margin tends to be less than 28.5¢ when bean supplies are large.

How are the tables used? **Follow this example** for practice, using the first table. If soybeans are $7.00 per bushel and if soybean oil is 23¢ per lb., what will be the estimated soybean meal price? Answer: $199 — found by going vertically on the 23¢ column, and horizontally on the $7.00 row to the square where the two meet at $199.

Another example — but this time it will be necessary to interpolate to get the answer. If soybeans are $6.95 and if soybean oil is 23.5¢, what will be the estimated soybean meal price? Answer: $194.25. Most times it will be necessary to use interpolation to find the meal price because it seldom happens that the oil price will be at the even cent e.g. 24¢ or that the bean price will be at the even dime e.g. $7.90.

Look more closely at the first table. You will notice that the table is set up for soybean oil prices from 17¢ to 28¢ and the soybean prices range for $5.60 to $8.00, in increments of 10¢. This table will cover about 80% of your needs. But there will be times when extreme prices occur, such as in the crop year 1983/84 — so this table would not be sufficient to handle them. Therefore, a second table with the extreme prices on it will be needed.

Look at the second table. Note that the soybean oil prices range from 23¢ to 43¢ and the soybean prices from $5.00 to $14.00.   Note, too, that the bean prices are in increments of 50¢ — this makes interpolation a bit more difficult.

Try this example. If soybean oil is 39.5¢ and if soybeans are $9.30, what will be the estimated soybean meal price? Answer - $220.7.   As mentioned before, this table will be used for extreme prices when soybeans are in tight supply — but the first table will cover about 80% of your normal needs.

How can these tables be used? One use is for working with the highest and lowest price tables from Parts 1 and 2.   **For example,** suppose you obtained from the tables in Part 1 that the estimated highest price for soybeans would be $7.80.   You might wonder, "What will be the meal price when beans reach $7.80?" Let's suppose oil at that moment was 22¢ and you figure it may go up another couple of cents with the bean price increase; so you use 24¢ on the tables with $7.80 for the beans, to get $230 for the estimated meal price.   What you are doing here is using the "What If?" method to help you in your forecasting.

Just to expand the example above a bit more, suppose after having obtained the $230, you figured that meal was more in demand than oil, and therefore could easily go another $20 higher, to maybe $250 — what would be the price of oil then? By moving along the line of the $7.80 price, you come to $249 which is close enough.   Looking vertically, you will see that oil will be 20¢ when meal is $249.

You could also find an estimated soybean price.   Suppose you were thinking that oil and meal prices would decline at the coming harvest, and you believed that oil would fall to about 20¢ and meal would decline to about $200, what would be the price of soybeans then? By looking vertically on the 20¢ column until you come close to $200, you will see that you are in the row for $6.70 for the soybean price.

Sometimes a meal/oil spread can be detected from the tables.   Follow these examples for practice.

Example: soybeans are $8.00, oil is 21¢ — then the estimated soybean meal price is $253.   But suppose the actual price for meal on the board at that time was $243, $10 less than the tables estimated.   That could mean two things: (1) the prices are out of line, and so are ripe for a spread or (2) the crush margin has fallen drastically.   The correct move should be to contact your broker and ask him to find the crush margin for that time — and if there is no problem there, one could take a spread by buying soybean meal/selling soybean oil.   Prices tend to come back into proper relationship fairly quickly.

No doubt you will find ways to use the tables for your own investigations and forecasts which may be applied to your own particular situations — not only with the two tables here but also with the tables immediately following.

ESTIMATED SOYBEAN MEAL PRICE

SOYBEAN PRICE	17¢	18¢	19¢	20¢	21¢	22¢	23¢	24¢	25¢	26¢	27¢	28¢	
8.00	$273	$268	$263	$258	$253	$248	$243	$239	$234	$229	$224	$219	8.00
7.90	268	263	259	254	249	244	239	234	229	224	219	214	7.90
7.80	264	259	254	249	244	239	235	230	225	220	215	210	7.80
7.70	259	254	250	245	240	235	230	225	220	215	210	206	7.70
7.60	255	250	245	240	235	231	226	221	216	211	206	201	7.60
7.50	251	246	241	236	231	226	221	216	211	206	202	197	7.50
7.40	246	241	236	231	227	222	217	212	207	202	197	192	7.40
7.30	242	237	232	227	222	217	212	207	202	198	193	188	7.30
7.20	237	232	227	223	218	213	208	203	198	193	188	183	7.20
7.10	233	228	223	218	213	208	203	198	194	189	184	179	7.10
7.00	228	223	218	214	209	204	199	194	189	184	179	174	7.00
6.90	224	219	214	209	204	199	194	190	185	180	175	170	6.90
6.80	219	214	210	205	200	195	190	185	180	175	170	166	6.80
6.70	215	210	205	200	195	190	186	181	176	171	166	161	6.70
6.60	210	206	201	196	191	186	181	176	171	166	162	157	6.60
6.50	206	201	196	191	186	182	177	172	167	162	157	152	6.50
6.40	201	197	192	187	182	177	172	167	162	158	153	148	6.40
6.30	197	192	187	182	178	173	168	163	158	153	148	143	6.30
6.20	193	188	183	178	173	168	163	158	154	149	144	139	6.20
6.10	188	183	178	174	169	164	159	154	149	144	139	134	6.10
6.00	184	179	174	169	164	159	154	150	145	140	135	130	6.00
5.90	179	174	170	165	160	155	150	145	140	135	130	125	5.90
5.80	175	170	165	160	155	150	146	141	136	131	126	121	5.80
5.70	170	166	161	156	151	146	141	136	131	126	121	117	5.70
5.60	166	161	156	151	146	142	137	132	127	122	117	112	5.60
	17¢	18¢	19¢	20¢	21¢	22¢	23¢	24¢	25¢	26¢	27¢	28¢	

SOYBEAN OIL PRICE

ESTIMATED SOYBEAN MEAL PRICE

SOYBEAN PRICE	43¢	42¢	41¢	40¢	39¢	38¢	37¢	36¢	35¢	34¢	33¢	32¢	31¢	30¢	29¢	28¢	27¢	26¢	25¢	24¢	23¢	SOYBEAN PRICE
14.00	413	417	422	427	432	437	442	447	452	457	461	466	471	476	481	486	491	496	501	505	510	14.00
13.50	390	395	400	405	410	415	420	425	429	434	439	444	449	454	459	464	469	473	478	483	488	13.50
13.00	368	373	377	383	388	392	397	402	407	412	417	422	427	432	437	441	446	451	456	461	466	13.00
12.50	346	351	356	360	365	370	375	380	385	390	395	400	405	409	414	419	424	429	434	439	444	12.50
12.00	324	328	333	338	343	348	353	358	363	368	372	377	382	387	392	397	402	407	412	417	421	12.00
11.50	301	306	311	316	321	326	331	336	340	345	350	355	360	365	370	375	380	384	389	394	399	11.50
11.00	279	284	289	294	299	303	308	313	318	323	328	333	338	343	348	352	357	362	367	372	377	11.00
10.50	257	262	267	271	276	281	286	291	296	301	306	311	316	320	325	330	335	340	345	350	355	10.50
10.00	235	239	244	249	254	259	264	269	274	279	283	288	293	298	303	308	313	318	323	328	332	10.00
9.50	212	217	222	227	232	237	242	247	251	256	261	266	271	276	281	286	291	295	300	305	310	9.50
9.00	190	195	200	205	210	214	219	224	229	234	239	244	249	254	259	263	268	273	278	283	288	9.00
8.50	168	173	178	182	187	192	197	202	207	212	217	222	227	231	236	241	246	251	256	261	266	8.50
8.00	146	150	155	160	165	170	175	180	185	190	194	199	204	209	214	219	224	229	234	238	243	8.00
7.50	123	128	133	138	143	148	153	158	162	167	172	177	182	187	192	197	202	206	211	216	221	7.50
7.00	101	106	111	116	121	125	130	135	140	145	150	155	160	165	170	174	179	184	189	194	199	7.00
6.50	79	84	89	93	98	103	108	113	118	123	128	133	138	142	147	152	157	162	167	172	177	6.50
6.00	57	61	66	71	76	81	86	91	96	101	105	110	115	120	125	130	135	140	145	150	154	6.00
5.50	34	39	44	49	54	59	64	69	73	78	83	88	93	98	103	108	113	117	122	127	132	5.50
5.00	12	17	22	27	32	36	41	46	51	56	61	66	71	76	81	85	90	95	100	105	110	5.00
	43¢	42¢	41¢	40¢	39¢	38¢	37¢	36¢	35¢	34¢	33¢	32¢	31¢	30¢	29¢	28¢	27¢	26¢	25¢	24¢	23¢	

SOYBEAN OIL PRICE

SOYBEAN PRICE

SECTION B
TO FIND THE ESTIMATED
SOYBEAN MEAL PRICE

The next graph and two tables will also find the estimated soybean meal price — but from a different perspective.

The tables in this section will use the value of soybean oil in a bushel of soybeans, as the basis for estimating the soybean meal price. There are approximatly 11 pounds of soybean oil in a bushel of soybeans. The equation for calculating the % value of the soybean oil is as follows: 11 × the price of soybean oil per lb. divided by the soybean price × 100. **Example:** If soybean oil is 24.3¢, and if soybeans are $7.52, what is soybean oil's value expressed as % of the soybean price? The equation is: 11 × 24.3 ÷ 752 × 100 = 35.5%. (note that the soybean price was written in cents). But to save you the trouble of figuring out the percentage, a convenient graph is provided to do the job.

Look at the graph "The % value of the soybean oil in an bushel of soybeans". Follow this example on the graph. **Example:** If soybeans are $8.00 per bushel and if soybean oil is 24¢ per lb., what % value is the soybean oil of the soybean price? Answer — about 33%, found by looking horizontally from $8.00 and vertically from 24¢. You can also play the "What If?" game, such as "What if soybeans decline to $6.00 at harvest and if the % value of oil falls to 30%, what will be the price of soybean oil?" Answer — about 16.4¢. Or, "What if soybean oil is 29¢ and if its % value is expected to rise to 41%, what will be the soybean price?" Answer — about $7.78.

Look at the first table "Estimated soybean meal price". Along the bottom (and the top) are the % values of soybean oil which you can get from the graph, or calculate them using the equation. Along the vertical sides are soybean prices, in increments of 10¢. This table will cover 80% of your needs. A second table will be used for extreme prices which occur once in a few years.

Example: (Follow this on the graph and tables). If soybean oil is 24¢ per lb. and if soybeans are $8.00 per bushel, What will be the estimated price of soybean meal.? **Step 1:** Using the graph vertically from 24¢ and horizontally from $8.00 — you get 33% (this means that 33% of the $8.00 soybean price belongs to the soybean oil's share i.e. $2.64). **Step 2:** Using the table, look vertically from 33% and horizontally from $8.00 — you get $239 as the estimated soybean meal price.

At this point you are wondering, "Why go to all the trouble of finding the % value when I can get the same answer from the first set of tables more quickly?" It is true that you will find the meal price quicker in the first tables. But the % value method opens up a new avenue of possibilities and investigation because you are thinking quantitatively; that is, you are thinking of the portion of the soybean price which belongs to the soybean oil e.g. 33% — whereas, in the first tables, you thought of soybean oil's price only e.g. 24¢.

But note this. Soybean oil's price will change for two reasons. The first reason is the familiar one — which is this: when soybean prices rise or fall, soybean oil's price will rise of fall in unison. We see that happening every day. But the second reason is more subtle. It is this: a change in the % value of soybean oil will cause a change in its price, even though the soybean price itself does not change. **For example**, suppose the soybean price was $7.50 and soybean oil was 28¢, which makes the oil a 41% value of the soybean price. Now suppose the % value changed to 39% but the soybean price remained constant — the price of soybean oil would now be 26.6¢, a decline of 1.4¢ with no change in the bean price. Also, in this example, because the oil's share of the bean price has decreased, the meal's share would increase in proportion. In the example here, the meal price would have increased from $197 to $204. All of which happened with no change in the soybean price.

This subtle change in the oil % value will help you to get a better fix on the meal price. **For example**, suppose the time is August, and soybeans are $8.00 and the oil is at 39% value. You have consulted the tables in parts 1 and 2 and have forecast a Nov. low of $6.90 for beans. (follow this in the tables for practice). With oil at 39%, the soybean meal price would be $187 in Nov. But suppose the crop of soybeans this particular year was large, giving an increased carryover — then you would be correct to lower the 39% value by a couple of points to 37% in Nov. Looking under the 37%, in the $6.90 row, you will get $193 as the new estimated meal price in November. You can see in this example that meal's price was changed twice: once by the decline in the bean price, and once by the change in oil's % value. Soybean oil's % value will often decrease at harvest if the crop is large, just as the example indicated.

What has been the history of the % value of soybean oil? What has been its range? From the crop year 1975/76 to 1983/84 the range has been from a low of 32% to a high of 44%, with an average of about 37% — until 1984 when soybean oil supplies became tight and the percentage value shot up to 49.5%

Please examine the last table in this set — for estimating the soybean meal price. Across the bottom (and the top) you will see % soybean oil values from 28% to 48%. This table is for those occasional years when there are extreme prices in the soybean complex. Along the sides you will see soybean prices ranging from $5.00 to $13.50, in increments of 50¢. You will need to interpolate here quite often to find the meal estimated price. The previous table, though, is easier to use and will be used for about 80% of your estimates.

40

THE % VALUE OF THE SOYBEAN OIL IN A BUSHEL OF SOYBEANS

SOYBEAN PRICES PER BUSHEL

SOYBEAN OIL PRICE PER POUND

41

ESTIMATED SOYBEAN MEAL PRICE

	31%	32%	33%	34%	35%	36%	37%	38%	39%	40%	41%	
8.00	$246	$242	$239	$235	$231	$228	$224	$221	$217	$214	$210	8.00
7.90	243	239	236	232	229	225	221	218	214	211	207	7.90
7.80	239	236	233	229	226	222	219	215	212	208	205	7.80
7.70	236	233	230	226	223	219	216	212	209	206	202	7.70
7.60	233	230	227	223	220	216	213	210	206	203	200	7.60
7.50	230	227	224	220	217	214	210	207	204	200	197	7.50
7.40	227	224	221	217	214	211	207	204	201	198	194	7.40
7.30	224	221	218	214	211	208	205	201	198	195	192	7.30
7.20	221	218	215	211	208	205	202	199	195	192	189	7.20
7.10	218	215	212	209	205	202	199	196	193	190	186	7.10
7.00	215	212	209	206	202	199	196	193	190	187	184	7.00
6.90	212	209	206	203	200	196	193	190	187	184	181	6.90
6.80	209	206	203	200	197	194	191	188	185	181	178	6.80
6.70	206	203	200	197	194	191	188	185	182	179	176	6.70
6.60	203	200	197	194	191	188	185	182	179	176	173	6.60
6.50	200	197	194	191	188	185	182	179	176	174	171	6.50
6.40	197	194	191	188	185	182	179	177	174	171	168	6.40
6.30	193	191	188	185	182	179	177	174	171	168	165	6.30
6.20	190	188	185	182	179	177	174	171	168	166	163	6.20
6.10	187	185	182	179	176	174	171	168	166	163	160	6.10
6.00	184	182	179	176	174	171	168	166	163	160	158	6.00
5.90	181	179	176	173	171	168	165	163	160	158	155	5.90
5.80	178	176	173	170	168	165	163	160	157	155	152	5.80
5.70	$175	$172	$170	$167	$165	$162	$160	$157	$155	$152	$150	5.70
	31%	32%	33%	34%	35%	36%	37%	38%	39%	40%	41%	

SOYBEAN PRICE PER BUSHEL

THE VALUE OF THE SOYBEAN OIL IN A BUSHEL OF SOYBEANS, EXPRESSED AS % OF THE SOYBEAN PRICE

ESTIMATED SOYBEAN MEAL PRICE

	48%	47%	46%	45%	44%	43%	42%	41%	40%	39%	38%	37%	36%	35%	34%	33%	32%	31%	30%	29%	28%	
13.50	312	318	324	330	336	342	348	354	360	366	372	378	384	390	396	403	409	415	421	427	433	13.50
13.00	301	307	312	318	324	330	336	341	347	353	359	364	370	376	382	388	393	399	405	411	417	13.00
12.50	289	295	300	306	312	317	323	328	334	339	345	350	356	362	367	373	378	384	389	395	401	12.50
12.00	278	283	288	294	299	304	310	315	320	326	331	336	342	347	352	358	363	368	374	379	384	12.00
11.50	266	271	276	281	287	292	297	302	307	312	317	322	328	333	338	343	348	353	358	363	368	11.50
11.00	255	259	264	269	274	279	284	289	294	299	303	308	313	318	323	328	333	338	343	348	352	11.00
10.50	243	248	252	257	262	266	271	276	280	285	290	294	299	304	308	313	318	322	327	332	336	10.50
10.00	231	236	240	245	249	254	258	263	267	271	276	280	285	289	294	298	303	307	312	316	320	10.00
9.50	220	224	228	233	237	241	245	249	254	258	262	266	271	275	279	283	287	292	296	300	304	9.50
9.00	208	212	216	220	224	228	232	236	240	244	248	252	256	260	264	268	272	276	280	284	288	9.00
8.50	197	200	204	208	212	216	219	223	227	231	235	238	242	246	250	253	257	261	265	269	272	8.50
8.00	185	189	192	196	199	203	206	210	214	217	221	224	228	231	235	239	242	246	249	253	256	8.00
7.50	174	177	180	184	187	190	194	197	200	204	207	210	214	217	220	224	227	230	234	237	240	7.50
7.00	162	165	168	171	174	178	181	184	187	190	193	196	199	202	206	209	212	215	218	221	224	7.00
6.50	150	153	156	159	162	165	168	171	174	176	179	182	185	188	191	194	197	200	202	205	208	6.50
6.00	139	142	144	147	150	152	155	158	160	163	166	168	171	174	176	179	182	184	187	190	192	6.00
5.50	127	130	132	135	137	140	142	144	147	149	152	154	157	159	162	164	166	169	171	174	176	5.50
5.00	116	118	120	122	125	127	129	131	134	136	138	141	142	145	147	149	151	154	156	158	160	5.00
	48%	47%	46%	45%	44%	43%	42%	41%	40%	39%	38%	37%	36%	35%	34%	33%	32%	31%	30%	29%	28%	

SOYBEAN PRICE PER BUSHEL

THE VALUE OF THE SOYBEAN OIL IN A BUSHEL OF SOYBEANS, EXPRESSED AS % OF THE SOYBEAN PRICE

43

WHAT IS AN AVERAGE SOYBEAN CROP YEAR?

The following information is the average of the years 1978/79 to 1983/84

Acres planted	68.2 million
Acres harvested	66.7 million
Yield	29.3 bu. per acre
Beginning stocks	277 million bushels
Production	1959 million bu.
Total supply	2236 million bu.
Domestic use	1144 million bu.
Exports	824 million bu.
Total use	1968 million bu.
Carryover	267 million bu.
Carryover as % of use	13.6%
Year's highest price	$8.65 (nearest month contract)
Date of highest price	June 1st
Year's lowest price	$6.26 (nearest month contract)
Date of lowest price	Oct. 24th

Also Available Through Windsor Books:

Corn Trading and Hedging by William Grandmill...$34.95

And

The Professional Trading System by R.C. Allen...$45.00
How To Build A Fortune In Commodities by R.C. Allen...$25.00
How To Triple Your Money Every Year
With Stock Index Futures by George Angell...$39.95
Optimal Commodity Investing by Gary Antonacci...$35.00
Megaprofit Commodity Methods by Robert Barnes...$69.95
Techni-Seasonal Commodity Trading by Everet H. Beckner...$65.00
The Taurus Method by Michael Chisholm...$75.00
The Colver Trading Method by Jay Colver...$50.00
Advanced Commodity Spread Trading by Harold Goldberg...$65.00
An Aggressive Campaign For Automatic Commodity
Trading by Joseph P. Hadad...$65.00
Advanced Commodity Trading Techniques by J. D. Hamon...$65.00
Eight New Commodity Technical Trading Methods by J. D. Hamon...$75.00
Breakthroughs In Commodity Technical Analysis by J.D. Hamon...$65.00
Inflation Profit Formula by J. D. Hamon...$50.00
High-Profit/Low-Risk Options Strategies by Humphrey Lloyd...$34.95
The Master Trading Formula by Donald S. Mart...$100.00
You Can't Lose Trading Commodities (New Edition) by Robert F. Wiest...$50.00
How I Made $1,000,000 Trading Commodities Last Year by Larry Williams...$50.00
Sure Thing Commodity Trading: How Seasonal
Factors Influence Commodity Prices by L. Williams & M. Noseworthy...$50.00

WINDSOR BOOKS
Box 280
Brightwaters, N.Y. 11718